Enjoy San Diego!
Andrew Hudson

Petco Park (2004) in downtown, a baseball park for the San Diego Padres.

About the Author

Andrew Hudson is a San Diego-based photographer who has published 14 books. His local books include **PhotoSecrets San Diego**—winner of the Grand Prize in the 1999 National Self-Published Book Awards—and **The Magic of Balboa Park**—winner of the 2000 Benjamin Franklin Award for Best Coffee-Table/Gift Book and the 2000 Book of the Year Award for Fine Art and Photography, 2nd place.

Born in England, Andrew lives in the Rancho Peñasquitos area of San Diego with his wife, Jennie, their children, Redford and Roxanne, and dog, Panang.

All photos by Andrew Hudson, © 1999–2007, except the following:
Pages 8, 10 (3), 57 and 64: Ron Gordon Garrison. © 1999–2007 Zoological Society of San Diego. All rights reserved. Reproduced with permission.
Pages 19, 20, 21: Bob Couey. Copyright © 1999–2007 Sea World, Inc. All rights reserved. Reproduced by permission.
Page 60 (2): Jerry Schad. © 1999–2007 Jerry Schad. All rights reserved.
Page 61: Jim Bremner. © 1999–2007 DesertUSA Magazine. DesertUSA.com

Published by:
Photo Tour Books, Inc.
9582 Vista Tercera
San Diego, CA 92129
Tel: 858-780-9726
phototourbooks.com

Distributed to the trade by:
National Book Network (NBN)
Tel: 800-462-6420.

Paperback:
978-0-9653087-8-6
(ISBN-10: 0-9653087-8-2)
Hardcover:
978-0-9653087-7-9
(ISBN-10: 0-9653087-7-4)

First edition, eighth printing, 2007.
Copyright © 1999–2007 Andrew Hudson / Photo Tour Books, Inc. All rights reserved. Designed on a Mac, published in San Diego, printed in Korea.

Dedicated to my wonderful little family — Roxy, Redford and Jennie. I love being together with you.

These books make great welcome gifts and corporate amenities. For quantity discounts call 858-780-9726. Stock photos also available.

Front cover: San Diego Bay. Back cover and above: Oceanside Pier. Opposite: Ocean Beach Pier. Endpapers (hardcover): Petco Park; Flower Fields of Carlsbad.

A Photo Tour of
San Diego

By
Andrew Hudson

Contents

The USS Midway, a naval aircraft carrier from 1945 to 1992 and now a floating museum.

Bai Yun is one of the Zoo's three giant pandas

San Diego Zoo

"A zoo is just about the most fascinating place in the world."
—Dr. Harry Wegeforth, founder of the San Diego Zoo.

The 'World-Famous' San Diego Zoo is the city's best-known attraction, and one of the largest zoos in the world. San Diego's ideal climate allows the animals to be displayed outdoors all year round.

One of the Zoo's most famous residents is Mei Sheng, a male panda cub born at the park in August 2003. He was the second panda to be born and survive in the United States. The first was his half-sister, Hua Mei, who was born at the San Diego Zoo in 1999, went to China, and has since had twins. Mei Sheng and his parents, Bai Yun and Gao Gao, are treated in San Diego as VIPs—Very Important Pandas.

Other highlights of the Zoo include the largest koala colony outside of Australia, Galápagos tortoises, two of the world's largest aviaries, plus polar bears, hippos, gorillas, orangutans, and tigers. The Zoo is also a botanical paradise, with over 6,500 varieties of plants providing shade and animal food.

Sumatran orangutan

Queensland koala

North Chinese leopard

Damara Zebra

River Hippopotamus

Balboa Park

"Balboa Park is one of the largest, most unusual and strikingly beautiful parks in the world." —John Nolen, City Planner, 1926.

With more museums, architecture, flora and fauna than any other city park in the world, Balboa Park is the gem of San Diego. The 1,200 acres contain tree-lined lawns, rugged canyons, hiking trails, golf courses, fifteen museums, and the San Diego Zoo.

The park was established in 1868, as a contemporary of New York's Central Park (1857) and San Francisco's Golden Gate Park (1870).

The park came of age in 1915 when a world exposition was held here to celebrate the opening of the Panama Canal. For the event, the park was named after the first European to cross Panama—Balboa Nuñez de Balboa.

On New Year's Day, 1915, a fireworks display in Balboa Park concluded with a flaming sign, "The Land Divided—The World United—San Diego the First Port of Call."

Architect Bertram Goodhue created a fantasy city using the best of Spanish-Colonial architecture. The romantic and evocative buildings were greatly admired and inspired much of Southern California's Spanish look.

A second exposition in 1935 added more buildings. The buildings of both expositions now house a complex of museums second in number only to Washington's Smithsonian Institution. Lovingly restored, the buildings are now listed as a National Historic Landmark.

Balboa Park contains a variety of trees and shrubs, many of which were planted in the 1890s by horticulturist Kate Sessions, the "Mother of Balboa Park". Today there are over 15,000 trees of over 350 different species, the majority of which are not native to San Diego.

Balboa Park

The Bea Evenson Fountain (1972), Balboa Park

Casa del Prado (1915), Balboa Park

Alcazar Garden and the California Tower (1915), Balboa Park

A fountain in Copley Plaza, Balboa Park

The Botanical Building (1915), Balboa Park

Shamu entertains the crowd at SeaWorld San Diego

SeaWorld

One of California's most popular tourist attractions, SeaWorld San Diego Adventure Park always makes for an entertaining day out. The big star, literally, is Shamu, a 4-ton killer whale who stars in *The Shamu Adventure*, one of the park's several acrobatic and educational marine life shows.

Opened in 1964, this was the first SeaWorld in the U.S. Highlights include polar bears in *Wild Arctic*, high-jumping dolphins in *Dolphin Discovery*, and spectacular fireworks during *Rockin' Summer Nights*, the park's summertime entertainment lineup. You can even *Dine with Shamu* at a poolside buffet only feet from the killer whales. If you order raw fish, be careful who you show it to!

Many of the performing animals try their best to soak spectators but the crowds keep coming back. They just have a whale of a good time!

Killer whales, SeaWorld

Sea lion and trainer, SeaWorld

Polar bears in the Wild Arctic exhibit, SeaWorld

Manchester Grand Hyatt (1992) and Marriott Marina (1987) hotels

Downtown

"I thought San Diego must be a Heaven on Earth…
It seemed to me the best spot for building a city I ever saw."
—*Alonzo Horton, 1867.*

Renovated and rejuvenated, downtown San Diego bustles with elegant restaurants in Victorian-era buildings, colorful shops in festive malls, museums on historic ships, and a convention center overlooking a sailboat marina.

San Diego's city center was founded in 1850 by William Heath Davis and developed in 1867 by Alonzo Erastus Horton, the "Father of San Diego". The area around Fifth Avenue boomed in the 1880s, becoming home to saloons, bordellos and gunslinger Wyatt Earp. Today the entire 16-½ block area known as the "Gaslamp Quarter" is on the National Register of Historic Places. The buildings have been restored and now house trendy bars and Italian restaurants.

In 2004, two new attractions were added to downtown San Diego: the $474 million PETCO Park, home of the San Diego Padres baseball team; and the USS Midway, a naval aircraft carrier from 1945 to 1992, now converted to a floating museum.

San Diego Trolley (1981) and the Harbor Club (1992)

Horton Plaza (1985)

Santa Fe Depot (1915) and the First National Bank building

County Administration Center (1938)

The Star of India (1863)

Emerald Plaza (1991) and Seaport Village (1980)

The Louis Bank of Commerce Building (1888) in the Gaslamp Quarter

Petco Park (2004), a new baseball park in downtown, home to the San Diego Padres.

Hotel del Coronado

"We ought to build a hotel…
the brightest…smartest hostelry on any coast."
—Elisha Babcock to fellow-founder Hampton Story, 1885.

A fairy-tale American castle, the lavish Hotel del Coronado is the largest wooden oceanside hotel on the West Coast. Built in 1888, 'The Del', as it is commonly known, is the last seaside resort remaining from California's opulent Victorian age. It is a National Historic Landmark.

The choice of 14 U.S. Presidents and numerous celebrities, The Del is probably most remembered as the place where Marilyn Monroe frolicked on the beach with Jack Lemmon and Tony Curtis in Billy Wilder's 1959 film, *Some Like It Hot.*

The hotel anchors the island-city of Coronado, across the bay from San Diego. Half the island is a major naval base, home port to several aircraft carriers. With its charming homes and palm-lined avenues, Coronado has more retired admirals than any other city in the country.

Hotel del Coronado (1888)

Hotel del Coronado in December

The San Diego skyline from Coronado.

The San Diego-Coronado Bay Bridge (1969)

The San Diego skyline at night, from Coronado

Cabrillo National Monument (est. 1913) with Coronado and San Diego behind

Cabrillo National Monument

"On this day, Thursday Sept. 28, 1542, we discovered a port, closed and very good." —Juan Rodríguez Cabrillo, in his log.

On the tip of Point Loma is one of the country's most visited National Monuments. A memorial to San Diego's 'discoverer', Cabrillo National Monument has great views of the Bay, as well as two lighthouses, a whale-watching station, a hiking trail, and several tide pools.

A 14-foot sandstone statue depicts Juan Rodríguez Cabrillo who, in 1542, was the first European to discover San Diego Bay and today's Californian coast. The heroic figure holds an explorer's pair of dividers and quadrant in one hand, and a conquistador's sword in the other.

Nearby are two lighthouses. Perched 422 feet above the ocean, the Old Point Loma Lighthouse is the highest ocean light in the country. However, it was often obscured by low clouds and a second light had to be built at the base of the hill.

Old Point Loma Lighthouse (1855)

The 'New' Point Loma Lighthouse (1891)

Old Point Loma Lighthouse atop Point Loma

Old Town San Diego State Historic Park

Old Town

"Thanks be to God, I have arrived at this port of San Diego.
It is beautiful to behold and does not belie its reputation."
—*Father Junípero Serra, 1769*

Old Town San Diego State Historic Park preserves the first permanent civilian settlement in California. The adobe houses (*casas*), originally built for the town's wealthy ranchers and merchants, have been restored and now house a feast of restaurants, museums and gift shops.

From 1822–72, during the Mexican and early American period, Old Town was the thriving center of San Diego. The most important resident was Pio Pico, Governor of California, who made San Diego the capital of California from 1824 to 1832. The site of Pico's house is now the Plaza del Pasado, a collection of restaurants around a festive courtyard.

Nearby, in Presidio Park, are the remains of the original Spanish fortress and mission, founded by Father Serra in 1769. Mission San Diego, relocated to Mission Valley in 1774, is the first of California's chain of 21 romantic Spanish missions.

The Casa de Reyes restaurant in Old Town.

The Theatre in Old Town

A Spanish fountain in Old Town

The Junípero Serra Museum (1929) in Presidio Park

Mission Basilica San Diego de Alcalá (est. 1769) in Mission Valley

Palm trees at sunset, La Jolla

La Jolla

"The Jewel of San Diego"

Pronounced in the Spanish style (lah-HOY-ya), La Jolla is one of California's most scenic and exclusive communities. Rugged cliffs, sculptured caves and intimate beaches line seven miles of serpentine shoreline, while Mediterranean architecture, galleries and restaurants line Prospect Street—the "Rodeo Drive of San Diego."

La Jolla is romantically interpreted from Old Spanish as "the jewel", giving this enchanting seaside community its deserved nickname—The Jewel of San Diego. The heart of the town is La Jolla Cove which, along with the surrounding coastline, was preserved by newspaper heiress and resident Ellen Browning Scripps.

La Jolla is a major research area, with the University of California at San Diego (UCSD), Scripps Institution of Oceanography (part of UCSD), and the Salk Institute for Biological Studies. The area is also the only native mainland location for one of the world's rarest trees, the Torrey pine.

Ellen Browning Scripps Park, La Jolla

43

La Jolla Cove

Sunny Jim Cave, La Jolla

Birch Aquarium at Scripps (1992) overlooks La Jolla and the Pacific Ocean

La Valencia Hotel (1926) in La Jolla

Wipeout Beach, La Jolla

Torrey pine trees on Broken Hill, Torrey Pines State Reserve

Para-gliders at Torrey Pines Glider Port

Beaches

Epitomizing the Southern California scene, the districts of Mission Beach, Mission Bay and Pacific Beach are popular for sunbathing, rollerblading, surfing, sailing and people-watching.

Mission Beach's Belmont Park, a restored oceanside amusement park, features the Giant Dipper, a bone-rattling wooden rollercoaster. Built in 1925 and recently restored, the Giant Dipper is one of the country's best small coasters and is the only rollercoaster on the National Register of Historic Places.

Mission Bay Park is a man-made 4,600-acre watersports playground with two islands, many coves and 17 miles of beaches. The park is popular for sailing, fishing, cycling, kite flying, water-skiing and jet-skiing.

Pacific Beach contains Crystal Pier, the only pier with a hotel. At the Crystal Pier Hotel you can sleep over the ocean in cottages dating from 1936.

Giant Dipper rollercoaster (1925) at Belmont Park in Mission Beach

Crystal Pier (1927) in Pacific Beach

Boardwalk and beach, Mission Beach

Crown Point, Mission Bay Park

Springtime at the Flower Fields of Carlsbad

North County

In 1933, Edwin Frazee started growing flowers in North County. Each spring, the "Flower Fields of Carlsbad" explode with over eight million ranunculus blooms. The fields are one of the largest such operations in the world and the only one open to the public.

In the 1880s, as the transcontinental railroad reached San Diego (via Los Angeles), the coastal resort cities of Carlsbad and Oceanside were developed. Dating from the 1890s, Oceanside Pier is the largest over-water pier in Southern California. It is so long that a golf cart is used to transport visitors to the popular Ruby's Diner at the far end.

Spanish priests and soldiers developed a road north from Mission San Diego in the late 1700s. Mission San Luis Rey de Francia was established in 1798 and became the largest and most successful of California's 21 missions. Known as the "King of the Missions" it was later used in the Zorro films by Walt Disney.

Giant ranunculus blossoms at the Flower Fields of Carlsbad

Oceanside Municipal Pier at sunset.

Mission San Luis Rey de Francia (est. 1798) in Oceanside

Sunset at the San Diego Wild Animal Park

Asian elephants at the San Diego Wild Animal Park (est. 1972).

The Julian Hotel (1897), Julian

San Diego's Backcountry

Almost in the center of San Diego County lies the 1870s gold-mining mountain town of Julian. Famous for its apple harvest and fall foliage, Julian lies 4,234 feet above sea level and makes a pleasant stop while visiting San Diego's backcountry.

More than a mile above sea level is Palomar Observatory. The massive 12-story white dome houses America's largest telescope, the 200 inch Hale Telescope, which has discovered galaxies and black holes.

Over half of San Diego is publicly owned land. Much of the mountainous midsection is protected as the 420,000-acre Cleveland National Forest, while the eastern mountain and desert area is protected as the largest state park in the contiguous United States, the 600,000-acre Anza-Borrego Desert State Park. Each spring following good rainfall, the desert floor lights up in a spectacular display of wildflowers.

Palomar Observatory (1948)

Desert sunflowers, Anza-Borrego Desert State Park

Barrel, hedgehog, and cholla cacti

Wildflowers in Anza-Borrego Desert State Park